At the Surprise Hotel

Manufactured in the United States of America.
Library of Congress Control Number: 2016945915

ISBN 978-1-56439-141-4 (paperback)

Designed and typeset by Megha Krishnan

At the Surprise Hotel

&

Other Poems

BARRY WALLENSTEIN

06/20/15

for PAT, DAVID + Matthew,

With Love,

Bay

Ridgeway Press

Detroit, MI

POETRY BOOKS

Tony's Blues, bilingual e-Book, Matthieu Baumier & Gwen Garnier-
   Duguy, 2014

Drastic Dislocations: New and Selected Poems, NY Quarterly Books, 2012

Tony's World, Birchbrook Press, 2010

The Tony Poems, Lyric Editions, 2001 [Illustrated by Chan Ky-Yut]

A Measure of Conduct, Ridgeway Press, 1999

The Short Life of the Five Minute Dancer, Ridgeway Press, 1993

Love and Crush, Persea Books, 1991

Roller Coaster Kid, T.Y. Crowell, 1982

Beast Is A Wolf With Brown Fire, BOA Editions, 1977

RECORDINGS OF POETRY

What Was, Was, Audioscope LC 12366 Suisa, 2015

Lucky These Days, Cadence Jazz Records CJR 1242; 2013

I Carry Your Heart, [BW's lyrics sung by Alexis Cole] Motema Records
   MTM 102, 2012

Euphoria Ripens, Cadence Jazz Records CJR 1210, 2008

Pandemonium, Cadence Jazz Records CJR 1194, 2005

Tony's Blues, Cadence Jazz Records CJR 1124, 2001

In Case You Missed It, SkyBlue Records, CD 106, 1995

Taking Off, AK-BA Records, 1040, 1982

Beast Is, AK-BA Records, 10200, 1978

ACKNOWLEDGMENTS

Grateful acknowledgment to the editors of the following journals in which many of these poems originally appeared: *Manhattan Review*; *BigCityLit; Kosmosis*; *Recours au Poème Sommaire*; *House Organ*; *The Cordite Poetry Review*; *La Traductiere*; *Presa*; Eco-Poetry.org; *New Contrast*; *Home Planet News*; *The Same.*

My gratitude is also extended to the residency provided by le Monastère, Centre des Monuments Nationaux, above the village of Saorge, France, where many of these poems were written.

Sincere thanks to Carol McDonald for her art work over many years.

This book is dedicated to the many inspiring jazz artists with whom I have collaborated.

CONTENTS

ENCOUNTERS

The Twilight Machine
Worker's Lament
A Minute's Something & Touch
Way Back Then
You Twirl and Dive
Love / The Telemarketer and the Janitor
Silent Dreams
Says the Boy with a Wart on his Nose
Speaking of Tanya
The Dispirited Lover
He Thinks Out Loud
That Was Then Forever
Swimming Towards 70
Vanity
Different Strokes
Sally Tells Suzie on their Way
Lyrics: The Devil Strikes Again
         The Split and the Healing
A Leap Beyond the Tyrants

DEPARTURES

The Child
Tomorrow
Exile in Old Age
His November / in the interim
Maturity
Prideful Creatures
Taking Names
Malignant
Elegy for a Man Who Hadn't an Easy Go/ Six Swipes at
Darkness
The Subject / A Dangerous Dream
Written in Pencil

Never to Get There
Thoughts of Home
The Old Dancer
Lyrics: For John Hicks
      The Farewell Trio on Tuesdays
Please, Listen to the Music
The Finale
Tony's Ghosts & Tony's Return
What Was, Was

At the Surprise Hotel
1 - 19

AT THE SURPRISE HOTEL

narrated by an anonymous member of the hotel staff

1.
Do not tremble upon arrival
at the Surprise Hotel.
Unlike places of horror,
this abode is benign,
nicely appointed, and
except in areas where less light is desired,
it's properly lit.

Carpets, not new, not frayed,
cover the ancient scars
caused by somebody dragging
something from somewhere
no one remembers.
Surely there are heroes here
deserving prizes.
Nevertheless —they are modest,
restrained at their varied stages.

So do not fear to fathom
the idea of a visit;
actualize it at the Surprise Hotel.

2.

No one is bruised on Sundays
at the Surprise Hotel
nor is any one citizen blessed
on purpose; but come Monday
the card players bust up the place
flipping their wigs,
sending their cards in the air.
The kings queens jacks aces all
sail off and then fall,
proving gravity a fine force
all the way to Tuesday.

3.
She dashed in — the darling of the place,
and her cousin came too,
a sparkly bird named Mona,
vernal, unbeaten, un-trodden, fresh as paint,
and the songwriters, the revelers, the men
who fix the pipes, all collapsed in love.

Lately, on blue days, they call out her name — Mona —
and the sound of it, the flush implied,
lifts their cloaks of blue, and suddenly
she's as violet vibrant as her cousin,
the unknown, the stick figure,
the darling of the place.

4.

A lout walked in
pressed a button
no one arrived.
He raved at the inattention
calmed himself down
pressed again
no one again.
The rave became a rant
against the hotel staff
standing about - ears stopped
our cool looks set
and ready for his ilk.

5.

At cocktail time one summer night
with the light lasting and the temperature cooling
and the moon too in a cooperative state,
a group of regulars
with time on their hands
and dinner not quite near
began quarreling out loud.

Why? A couple -- the man tall and sleek
and the woman also tall and sleek
and dressed in black with dark lips
slinked into the lobby, silent movie style.
One gent said – look at that,
and another laughed, and another grumbled,
while one sat stone-still as if star-struck
and spoke out loud
"you damn fools sitting there
didn't even see what just passed?"

6.
Adam, tall, buff, and tender of the bar,
wipes the circles
off the polished wood
after Rascal, as he's called,
stood up, glass in hand
and stumbled off the foot-rail,
in this last half hour of twilight
at the Surprise Hotel.

As light dims, he tumbles
into an unseen and tricky present tense;
where the brass rail's a bad memory
and the mistrusted messenger's fallen off his bike.
Rascal's here; the proof is in his silence
and his droppings.

7.

See the moon-glow change the shapes
across the west wall of room 305
occupied this night
by a traveler weary from the road.
He smokes his last cigarette,
opens the window to clear the air.
Then he, call him Tommy, looks over the parking lot
and drifts; he closes the window
on an updraft of conversation he's not part of.
In fact, he imagines himself no part
of any conversation at all.

8.
In the Lizard Lounge
the leather-cushioned booths
hold three across -- four tightly.
There the loafers, the juice friends,
and twilight runners,
sometimes sit and
try to improve their chatter.
The sucker punch senders,
the pratfall entertainers
the off-season aerial acts
all wait around as if in heaven
talking and listening to the music
in the lounge just off the lobby.

9.
This particular drop-by, part-time resident,
dressed for luxury, is for certain
one of the party of oddballs.
He's a glad hand with gravel,
tight fisted with gold.

Nelly says, "it's lucky for the staff
his stays are short and occasional."
When he does come back each time,
it's to room number two
and the curtains stay drawn.

He's tried in his slick way twice
to fool with Nelly
who bell-hops part time
and is often seen behind the bar
being playful – but she says scat.

Yes, he's tight fisted with the gold;
silver stays home with the cat.

10.
Nelly says,
"if he didn't stink sometimes,
you wouldn't know he's around."

She speaks of the guest in 508 —
never late for breakfast
never speaks
always tucks his napkin
neatly under his chin,
and when he stands after the meal,
his re-sets the table.

He tiptoes towards his room silently,
with the face of an abstract, slowly
over the rug as if measuring it —
well-dressed but radiating
a most peculiar odor.

"Still, there's worse in this world
than funk," Nelly says with a smile,
and it's known she prefers her woe
in thimble-sized glasses.

11.
The Masons were overbooked
at the Mayflower Hotel,
so the flow of conventioneers –
after a call or two or ten –
and consultations –
hopped on a mini-bus
and jolted along to the Surprise Hotel

where they milled about the entrance,
separate souls bound by a
secret sacred trust, ancient and long forgotten.
The wallets walked in,
and straight-faced the register took their names,
the date, previous address and occupation.

12.
Another afternoon, Françoise,
over here for a year,
told a group of listeners
how back home she'd climbed a mountain:
"We started out from the village,
then mounted higher all the way to the crest
past almond trees, fig trees and wild animals.
We walked as if on the clouds."

One new guest at the hotel, a shy fellow,
heard her story and fell in love
with the way she told it,
with her damaged teeth, brown eyes,
thin bare shoulders,
less-than-perfect posture –
her accent and her aroma – an unsettling scent.
This drove him past distraction
and into his small room off the lobby
where he remained 'til check out time.

13.
There's a commotion down in the lobby
by the front desk:
it's Friday and the crafty fellow
from room 403 speaks excitedly of rats,
a profusion of rats.
Last time it was wasps.
Each time he wants the bill burned.
"So, when did these alleged rats appear,
and can you show them to us or us to them?"

The aggrieved party lowers his voice –
he sees the rubberneckers bend in our direction
and semi-whispers,
"No, they've gone back into hiding."
Then he rolls up his sleeve and holds out
his left arm ravaged and scarred
with what look like festering rat bites.

14.

Suite 108 called down an emergency –
a plumbing problem –
what? how? when? – "NOW"
her outrage shrieked into the phone:
"in the middle of the shower,
my hair all soapy lather,
the cold water disappeared,
and I was almost scalded
and nearly slipped escaping from under
that burning hot water.
I was blinded by the blend of soap
and hair softener, my eyes still stinging
and the water won't turn off,
and a flood is overflowing from the bath
the steam so you can't see and
the towels floating into the entrance-way
and my robe is soaked."

The plumber, quickly summoned, arrives
alone. He's an amazingly small man,
no taller than 4 feet but well- proportioned,
his hands strong enough to bend a pipe.
But pipes weren't the problem.
At first, he must have frightened her,
his sweet head at eye level with her flood,
as if bobbing there.
He quickly released the drain, shut the faucet,
and sloshed his way out.
He left her sitting in a chair, toweling her hair;
she wears faux rhinestone tears
and a stuck-on goatee
and stares out the window over the trees
that provide shade to the parking lot.

15.
The resident of 109
speaks sometimes in a whisper
or pitches his voice real loud.
Some days he's private, other times less so.
Today he pretends indifference
to the mayhem across the hall.
This pose covers not his curiosity
running wild about the plumber.
His yearning is unknown to the plumber,
who, he quips, is a midget.

The plumber's reserve feels like a thorn
caught on his need like an itch,
so he tells this story aloud.
When young he killed toads
and then a little older and more sensitive,
he saved toads' lives endangered by the young
sadistic demons he ran with before.

He dreams if only this Plumber,
with an upper case P
could know him and his capacities –
where would they not sail?
But finished in 108, this man of the capital P,
never senses the current.

16.
There was to be a Jewish wedding on the 12th,
a grand affair in the large ballroom
off the Lizard Lounge,
catered from the outside.
The deposit had already been paid,
promises made in all directions.
He seemed happy – she seemed happy;
the in-laws on both sides were aflutter.
All was ready,
until the taxi ride in grid-lock
held up everything:
the couple was not there –
late or never ? – no one knew.

Back to the taxi: an Arab driving
and the groom in a tuxedo,
front seat to back seat:
"To what are you going?" –
"To the place of my wedding" –
"Ahh, wonderful" – sings the driver, and
"Where're you from?" asks the groom
"Palestine…"
"Ahh, so impossible; so terrible. Yes…
and the occupation's a stain on us"
"… and worse than a stain on us;
a total nightmare you know."
They agreed to stop for a drink
just eleven blocks from the hotel,
with so much traffic and the interest of talk.

After an hour in the bar neither
will ever forget, the groom calls the hotel:
"Sorry to be late – had to leave the cab
and walk – please tell Susan I'll see her tomorrow.
Might we change the date from the 12th to the 14th
and add four more place settings?
The family's name is Sanwar, Yehia Sanwar."

17.
The words for this surprise,
when they checked in for a two day stay, were:
incongruous, disgusting, beyond the law --
each word a scold
at them and the hotel too.

The man is overly large,
a mass of flesh – so the louts call him
fatso, pig, a ton of lard, an El Groso.
Voluminous as he is,
he dresses like a cool millionaire.
His accessories come from abroad.

His mate is lithe, sinewy – an impossible beauty
with lashes like the fins of fancy fish
shadowing amber eyes
and a smile so calm, so direct:
she's a rose petal on the arm of this giant.

It's the cliché of every hotel:
young enough to be his ..., but
it turns out they're in town for show business;
he's a singer – anything from grand opera
to scat, German lieder to blues.
She takes care of the details.

18.
One Wing of Surprise; William Burroughs Spent a Night

Within these single rooms along the west corridor
there hides what no one expects to see,
a Surprise wing where the less well-healed
stay for short spells – transients.

They never take dinner with the regulars
and they – normally single persons –
don't go out much, and when they do,
they go quickly:
one man always, mid-way out the exit,
points his hand westward with a twitch
as if the dowser's wand were in his mind,
but he returns empty each time;
another has a face marked by a losing battle,
and another, I won't go into it, is obscene
"beyond any possible vile act or practice."

What no one expects is the solitary writer
spending a week scribbling at the hotel:
He's not the voyeur we imagined or feared.
No, the staff loves him, and some of us read his books.

19.
She arrived within a bubble of silence,
a pleasant face burdened under a sack of grief.
The ream of paper she carried
would, one day, she aspires,
tell the story of her terrible loss
and maybe transform
or shift that loss to a station of her heart,
where it will rest and take a right shape
to calm herself and please her God.

Maybe – she says maybe with melody,
as if the word were her favorite –
she'll enter a nunnery where
in such tranquility she'll find even better words
to express how even this thing –
the sudden young death
can be felt and viewed as a blessing
in no need of disguise.

Nelly whispered to Adam one evening
after rubbing down the bar,
"that one – the woman who speaks
of quietude –loss and gain –
is wrestling with God."
"No," he said, "that match is long over."

Events

THE SOMMELIER SAYS

the wine is "light but complex,"
as the four at the table sit back
and swap smiles
around a bottle of best red –
in this polished tavern fronting
a grand boulevard.

Then the sommelier, smart suit and a slight bow,
praises the valley, the region, and the year,
when the damp of April
extended into May, joined with
arid June and parched July
to generate the sweetest grapes –
light but complex.

The diners sip and smile again,
having put to sleep the threat of riots.
The image of a mangled throat in the back alley
is obscured by the rhythm of the servers,
as they glide smoothly by each table -
complexity well-hidden within their grace.

ONE MORE ACCIDENTAL BIRTH

She didn't think to name her god, anything
so the god, being spiteful, developed a singular disposition,
and after years of spitting up and letting others
clean it up, this cantankerous, plotting,
half-baked, off-balanced creep
--they call him Split Wing the Undertaker—
filed down cities,
sent fires up spires,
in his will-o'-the-wisp time.

She questions: how to rid the land
of this scourge – this godling gone wrong?
She couldn't turn back time
or stop its forward progress,
but she could devise a trap
with wires and springs and rods of steel.
She tied a mirror to his skull,
and seeing inward so,
he lied down tired and died.

She knows now that when next
some great wind or shadow
enters her chamber at night,
the issue of that encounter
will be hugged and well minded
and with a name she'll never misspell.

AN EVENING SURPRISE

An assemblage of deadbeats,
assorted intellectuals and sex hounds
gather each month to relax
and un-figure the universal system.
This night they were all surprised.

It was mid-way through the party
when time began to speedball
an improvised release.
Even before that, though few knew,
there was blood on the sheets
and short bursts of laughter.

First, a prolonged kiss disarmed the lot,
and then the developing rapture
shook every single jaded soul.
A he and a she – as in the tabloids –
had taken themselves aside,
and disrobed almost hidden from view.

It was the *almost* that undid the imagined order;
the hand on the throat, erotic,
was observed;
the hand on the neck, sentimental,
was observed.
Confusion drove through the midnight hours.

By 2am, a sweetness,
tinged with the spite of fallen angels,
settled on the group; the wolves and wolverines
sobered up and exited in their various ways
with an assortment of smiles, new currency
clinking and suspect in their pockets.

MINA'S FROWN

tells us nothing about her heart;
the way she holds the knife,
knuckles white, lips blue and trembling,
frightens the children
gathered around the table.
Today the table is set badly.

By all appearances, Mina is a marvel –
seeing into the hearts of people,
regulating charts, running the shop,
and when the need arises,
she'll put on gloves to repair a gadget.
But today she seems frozen in her frown;
and the cloudy look on her steady face
seems about to turn stormy.

Could that stranger who spent an hour
a day ago – visiting the shop – have set her off?
We saw him from afar pacing,
stomping down his points.

Someone says he heard something
about debt finance, or finesse the bill,
and then she said, and he's sure he heard right,
"I'm closing," and she frowned,
locked the door, and turned on the radio.

HE TALKS TO CHARLIE

Enough about me,
now tell me about you.

[tiny pause]

What do you think about me?

[silence]

Listen: the 12 foot schooner out on the lake
is but a twig compared to the ship I sailed
as Captain Kidd,
an alias to hide a connection
with Lord Vicious – never my friend
but always close and a beauty.

Charlie, what's that faraway look as I speak?
Some critique grown in your skull?
My speech is not about me but you and us.
If I tell you what we ate and smoked there
on that blasted, shipwrecked island,
you'd love the story but be too occupied to respond.

But if you go on about your essay on pathos,
and how this high-toned, well-known
and on-time journal is about to publish
and pay well to print your title,
"The Wealth of Feeling,"
I'll surely stop you for the health of my mind.

Tell me more about your son
who fell off a wall protesting something –
your details were lost in the wind;
remember? we were talking in the wind
and soon it was to be my turn.
This much I heard: he's OK, alive and behaving.

The winds have died down, you devil,
and since you haven't answered my question
or given any indication of how I am
in your mind's eye, I'll talk to myself —
as if no one were sitting across from me
here on the patio these last few days.

MY DOG

Just now, after many years of bogus calm,
I've met my match in the shape of a dog,
an angry beast outside the barn I rent
just beyond the city lights.
This dog's an amazing creature,
five feet tall and wider than reason;
his jaw is tense and his teeth snap.
There's no way to know – ever –
when he'll relax or attack.

But I'll tame that mutt before I die,
medicate him with whispers,
sweet promises of greasy bones
and kinder dogs to learn from.
I'll lead him to fire plugs, places to aim at.
But, the guy who called me a dog
for some minor misdemeanor,
should step back –
and beware our fearful fangs.

HUNGRY BOY

Twelve might be his number,
but if thirteen were upstairs
he'd leap two at a time
to snatch the extra digit.

He demands the plural on every shore,
picks up everything rough or smooth
- sometimes twice – even thrice,
when beach combing or anywhere.

Flowers dissolve inside his mouth,
roses and phlox, lilies and poppies;
his saliva composts the weeds
jutting through his teeth.

He sits there in a mist, smoking,
and with a practiced finger,
removes a cinder from his left eye –
and then he chews on some prize.

He's both central and aside.
In want of shade and sunshine,
sitting on the edge of each,
eager, satisfied for only a moment, swinish.

Forever, he collects favors
red green and large;
a gobbler, a guzzler, a devourer,
incendiary – he burns himself out.

CLIMBING AMBITION

He knows only the sins of children, of wanting more and to be first.

He made friends easily – Betsy,
who built his last ladder, was a lover,
an artist who added platforms
every ten steps, as the climb went up.

Perched high above the ordinary strivers,
he rested, dreamt of more and the views above.
The dream powered his push
to the next level.

On the final shelf before the crest,
he demanded a pool with a diving board.
That's when Betsy bristled, slacked off at work,
and finally kissed his head goodbye.

The penultimate rung
suffered the pressure of his step-down
to go up higher –
then he heard the snap of wood – oh, Betsy.

UNPREPARED

One day his pet snake escaped.
He called him Slither from the start,
for the shape reminded him of a word
that had slipped away
before he could learn it.

He kept his doors unlocked – always
so anything could leave or intrude anytime.
He knew the patterns of the wind
and the faces of all the thieves
who otherwise might have crept around
but didn't.

He never adjusted the sails
on his homeward glide;
the breeze was just that steady,
but inches beneath the hull,
shadows drift and break
against the jagged stones.

SPOKEN BY A MAN DOWN ON HIS LUCK

I plead with old cheesy-face, man in the moon:
"Please, I've my back up against the wall
with not a chance in hell" –
he frowns at my phrases, turns impassive,

as I carry on about he
who cannot escape the dance
he stumbles through, a dance for animals –
excited red-faced and awkward.

The moon is dull and silent;
a cloud crosses its path,
and I'm in the dark again – pleading,
talking to a dolt / myself,

a mooncalf on this vacant field
filled only with stars,
their pricks of light illuminating little –
the lists of debts, the hard luck, no life-line.

THE FEARFUL FEARSOME BARBER

All that I have pivots
on what I have to do
to preserve my share of the currency,
not make the pile grow - necessarily
but at least, to guard it.
I ll protect that pile, be it with a fence,
a wall or a poisoned moat.
Forces would plunder, even bludgeon,
to change my situation.

I ve still work to do
here in this tonsorial palace:
another head to improve
with my clip clip and snip snip
and with razor in hand
make that head smooth and clean
right below the hairline, by the nape of the neck.
I adjust the mirror,
and the image comes clear;

MURDER IN THE RANKS

A dull-eyed woman with a bad dye job
begins to moan and swoon,
overcome by revolutionary bliss.
The one who hates her
has a blade half-hidden.
She too believes in the cause
but is less reverential.
They never quarrel outright
though each knows
the other's misguided
and would "go to lengths,"
as both moms say, to set matters right.

Meanwhile the revolution's caught fire,
borders are erased, populations thinned out,
purified, massacred.
The engines have stopped –
less noise, no fumes.
The tracks humankind
ran on for ages are twisted;
but where are they now –
the devotées –
on this lovely springtime morning?

Performance Poems

I.

THESE TIMES OF NEED

You need money honey
to grow money
on the fertile fields of plenty;
even on the fallow fields of want
some plots are richer than others,
and the well-fed tight fisted – they taunt.

Pity the crawling after radish
pity the gaunt.

Many acres won't yield
a thin dime's worth of wheat,
a sprig or anything; pity the crawling
too – after dollars and their chances.
The lives of these currencies are wild
speculation – into the devil's dances.

Pity the well this season gone dry
pity the well-digger his rationale sigh.

You need money honey
to grow money
out of itself – interest bearing,
every moment increasing
your pile, the store of cash,
wealth's illusion – fast imploding.

Pity not the dog whipped by its master
pity the master, his life a blur.

A new cousin's come to town:
buy her a hat, a scarf, a toy
to toy with. But without that money
you less-than-honey, take care:
she may ascend to the bus
and leave your lap the weight of loss.

Pity the roof, its shingles blown away,
pity the hallway where silence holds sway.

2.

PHONE CALLS TO MAKE [PHONE RINGS]

Call the butcher
to deliver beefsteak
many pounds prime
call the lemonade
call the editor – take my silver
take my gold
call the gunsmith
powder the muzzle
call the meter-reader
must have been drunk bleary-eyed
or criminal
call the priest of the seven veils
a kiss on the phone goodbye
call the lemonade
call the one who baits your heart
call the angels from out the dark
whispering low
call the lemonade
call the cobbler to do his best
call the doctor
the machine says—call back after
call the lemonade
call the weatherman
call the enemy where he rests
where he plots where he mourns
bring him 'round – debts cancelled
safe passage promised and delivered
call the lemonade
call the children
call the children
of those who've called before.

3.
THAT WAS THEN; NOW IS PAID FOR

Novocain Mary, lately out of stir,
balances on a bed's edge
and ponders the ways to rise.
Once vertical though listing, she slips from the room
and into the luxury of Handsome Harry –

his white, fully loaded, hand washed
four door Cadillac – 1980s Coupe-de-Ville –
faux leopard seat cushions
stereo surround sound and a sunroof
made of bomb-proof glass -- real glass --

Harry turns the silver key
a smooth click and a hum—
the quietest sound in silverdom.
They sail through the city;
with the clock on the dash on time.

In the bath sometimes Mary encourages a toy boat
to float in her direction.
She smiles at the recollection of her pleasures,
and watches expectantly as Harry drives the car
into the outer boroughs.

66 PARK AVENUE IN CHANGEABLE WEATHER

cuttle fish
from under a cloud-burst, a young couple
dashes into the first lobby they see -
66 Park Avenue - and it's warm,
and the doorman inhales their single sent,
their animated, wet and chilly aspect
as they shake the drops from hat and coat.
Bending, they smile up at the groomed kindness.

starfish
the doorman, Sam, with a plane blue jacket
and red bowtie, shiny dark trousers
with a silk stripe running down
to the tops of his shoes,
hands over a woolen blanket
and says "sit by the stove
and rest 'till you're dry."

viper fish
and they do, but everything changes
once Sam steps out on a break.
Outside the rain stops,
the sun shines, and the winds calm;
inside the couple – now dry and still –
imagine never leaving the lobby
or the comfort of the stove.

puffer fish
prepared well will kill no one,
and Sam, returned, has a dish in mind,
something savory for the young couple
to whom he's taken a definite shine;
but his plans are dashed by their absence.
He searches by the stove, the alcove, the hallways –
gone; even the stove's gone.

THE MAN IN THE MASK

When the markets fell in '08,
the middle class took a hit.
One individual, poorly shod now
and biting hard against his luck,
turned his desperation into action.
On a dark autumn day, in a flimsy mask,
he pointed his 45 magnum pistola
at a group of terrified bank tellers –
"hand over the high numbers
and look at me all the while steady
and believe me – one wrong move
and nobody gets outta here alive."

The cliché slipped by his lips unchecked
and sent a shiver down his shoulder
and beyond the bank.
His gun hand trembled
and dropped its weight.

The sudden clatter released the chatter
held in all those anxious throats.
Slowly, the lines broke
and the population, confused now,
pressed in.

TOWARDS EVENING

Three men stand by the end of a cigarette
which decorates the mouth of Melody
who could be their heart's desire.

Two of the three wish the guy to his right
were a little more friendly.
The third, glancing left,
wishes his closest mate were less friendly.

Finally three matches are struck;
Melody's face changes with the inhalation,
as the men stand still.

STREET SIGNS

On the corner, several road signs
bend around a post.
Arrow north reads
"Devils Design Street"
and the other points south
to "Nowhere Street."

A shot rings out from Immediate Alley,
and the action's caught on video:
the person at the crossroads, hesitates,
locked for minutes in mid-step
confused by the wrap of signs.
Street-smart and quick enough,
he ducks the shot that blasted all signs back to order.

Dusting himself off a little,
he looks up at the compass settings
and sets forth into Immediate Alley
with a zip in his step and a zap in his pocket
that the camera hadn't caught earlier.

FACES

The dog began speaking to me
but was too late –
I'd already turned the corner
and found my route.
Surely, I have my foibles,
periods of vanity
easily vexed,
but I'm mindful of the scars
on the faces of those around me;
I've known these faces a long time.

And then there are the smooth-faced wonders
the hypocrites who never talk like dogs,
never bark out warnings – never instruct.
They too should be wary of error, of mishap,
or pretend that way for practice.

THE BULLET COUNCILS THE HEAD

When I count to 3 – *on 3* –
take this hint – dodge quickly aside
and lower your head – duck!
I say this to save your life.

I know the man with the gun;
he practices daily –
by evenings too. Don't relax too much
now or in the coming weeks.

I don't know why he has you in his sights —
you seem a decent fellow,
and I know your face should remain whole.

He always presses the trigger at 4
and then I'm off in your direction
with no power to shift course
or do anything but strike – where?
where your brain is right now
and has been –
I don't want to touch it
or spit it onto yonder wall.

Listen to me – this is your bullet speaking –
high caliber and wishing you well.

ELSEWHERE

Here is one place – a comfort zone
with an accurate time piece,
a wool sweater for winter and
someone to love and in good health.

Elsewhere, the rocks on Elba
are being blasted by the sea.
Elsewhere the stones heat in the sun,
as the lizards hurry for shade or shadow.
Elsewhere stubble grows on the chin,
a woman takes something for yeast,
a child from a well-groomed family
practices filth; the year lapses into grief.

Elsewhere in autumn a young man
is taught a new language.
His tutor encourages studious time
and down time.
She pretends he's a master of the universe,
and he does build a city – on a small scale.
His iron hammer clangs on the anvil;
the sparks shoot to the stars.

MASTERY

Unable, at the start,
to do the love thing right,
he practiced stroke by stroke
and melting into whoever was by
slowly — as slowly as one
tip-toes forward and around
dripped honey circles
on the way to the jar.
Some sweet danger in every drop
until he's safe under the lid.

Unable, late in life,
to do the large thing right
he takes on the small
inch by inch — to do
dividing the inch by quarters,
eighths, many times over
into minutia.
Click by click of the needle
stitch by stitch by miniscule stitch —
then comes the day the fabric's done.

CHANCE PERFORMANCE

A white pillar of sand stands
close by the New Infirmary;
mica flecks, embedded there,
glint and shimmer.

The sand fly, despite her broken wing
and all that distance flown,
knows she s the luckiest moving object
in the territory.

POETRY WRITER

But it isn't easy, said Pooh to himself...
because Poems and Hums aren't things which you get,
they're things which get you.
And all you can do is to go to where they can find you.
a.a. Milne

I went first to an open field
on the broad side of a hill,
walking over heather and sticks,
ups and downs crests and dips,
and further up - scrubs and pines:
all the disorder that nature resembles.
Still, the hums didn't come.

Next, I visited a scholar
in his dark and book-filled den.
The brain was out, and I lit his pipe
and had a dream of letters dancing
and then bounding
on their way.

So where do these restless words scramble
to sing to rhyme – beneath a hum –?
On this hill, on this field of sun and shadow;
or it could be there, where the scribbler
sits upon the heather,
a feathered quill moving in his hand.

POETRY READER

*Reading it, however, with a perfect contempt for it, one
discovers in it after all, a place for the genuine.*
from "Poetry" by Marianne Moore

The reader walks the farm someone else planted;
he wanders between lost and found.
These are the difficulties.
Finally his eye settles on a bank of herbs:
lavender, rosemary, thyme, and
the frail leaves of mint;
marigolds decorate in-between
and in the beds along the rise.

This farm is a template:
in every rhythmic row of vegetables
are promises;
in every wish for berries
there's flourishing.
Even the sway of the scythe,
as it cuts away unwanted growth,
is an emblem – the joy within difficulty.

THE BODY AS POEM

Before you, the couplet –
body&being
form&spirit –
I was but a line of syllables almost lost
until joined by the you,
and should there be more lines added
to the life of the body
more of you into me –
the body well into the poem
growing in volume,
a quatrain perhaps or a sonnet,
yes I'll merge
my measures with yours,

as you take that metaphorical bite
of my prosaic neck.

ARS POETICA

He couldn't make the poem right,
so he lost weight instead –
to shape his harmony, his girth,
tighten everything
to please the eye of love,
before the journey home.

First he had to climb a hill,
create a new disposition,
lift a weight greater than his own
and move it upward
to a dizzy height –
dactyls to help him break the fall.

He was alone at the summit,
with a simple fridge and a single plate
and a morsel, and off to the side,
a scale to weigh his form,
a measure 'round the belt line,
a structure to be scanned.

At the end of the discipline
he'd slimmed down, first to a quatrain,
then to a couplet, but on closer look
he sees a few fat words, dead weight,
a burden on the whole;
it needs editing, a new regimen.

Encounters

THE TWILIGHT MACHINE

Alejandro sings in his sleep.
He comes to my browns, my red heart,
my store of references;
he loves my young eyes full time he says
and for all his family.

His daughter, Alejandra, calls out her needs:
my ears at the end of her voice
nearly fill with wax,
but the words slide beneath the barricade,
each one an insinuation.

Alejandro's family is large, wise and wild.
They invite me into their home
where I entertain with slight-of-hand,
do a conjuring trick or two,
magic enough to insure my stay.

At twilight, every day,
one from the group vanishes
while none of the remaining notice,
but each time their attention on the cards
and the way I move my hands increases.

After weeks of this – good food on the table,
wine, and the family appearing and disappearing
like ghosts on a string, like variegated angels –
Alejandra remains missing,
caught beyond my magic in the mists.

WORKER'S LAMENT

The very first day
I started cleaning at Virgil's villa,
I was terrified I'd break the crystal,
scratch the fine oak table
with the vacuum,
or damage the machine itself;
but on that same day, after one long look,
I feared most
being stripped by his daughter.

Virgil had a rough beard
and a bald head wrapped in a bandana.
I thought him a pirate
or a professional wrestler.
She looked like a '20s flapper,
a rosy face – natural skin.
She pointed to a room,
the one I shouldn't clean.
She left me that evening with a taste
stranger than my first fear.

A MINUTE'S SOMETHING

You have the slow eyes of an old man
and I do not, sitting here,
imagine you growing younger,
nor do I know the condition of your body.

OK, let's say you're clean
but with a mind slick enough to capture
some part of my fancy.
I could fall for that for a minute.

Close your eyes;
I won't pick your pocket.

TOUCH

a gift for hunger
as well as loneliness,
a wafer pure and secular.
Loam crawls with life,
clean as the wish
to send innocent arms
around innocent shoulders.
Arms or shoulders are candid and pure.

Touch: the harbinger of union,
the enduring condition
of a practiced heart,
a tonic for insult and confusion.

WAY BACK THEN

First I thought I'd faint, but I awoke instead
about 30 miles from the city
with the sea on my right
and her elbow (good fortune) on my left.

She pressed her thumb and middle fingers –
slightly oiled – on my upper spine
and drew them downwards
towards and onto the coccyx and
then ran those lubricated digits back up
to the neck and put on pressure and
then swiftly ran them down again
paused awhile – passionless –
and then slowly all the way back up.

In between then and now –
on and off – my back's been my enemy;
too many stones have been lifted;
some made it to the wall,
others not.
Now, I'd welcome that very masseuse –
if that's what she was, way back then.

YOU TWIRL AND DIVE

You twirl and dive in the sunlight
and then perhaps in moonlight
before misbehaving,
before settling into the rhythm
that suits you and your sulk
jolly as you sway on your way.

So, wonderful you, total you,
will you meet my request
to sing in my register,
follow closely the shifts of my chords,
low or rising up the staff
at this time of the day?

If we do this, rich as we are already,
we'll break the bank and celebrate
all that's come true – even the slips
and the grievances.
The forecast says lovely weather;
good news for our latter-day moves.

LOVE / THE TELEMARKETER AND THE JANITOR

They were so in love they forgot their places.
First one then the other took his then her
eye off the job;
with the janitor, the garbage mounted sculpturally.
Soon judges from the museum,
in concord with others in the know,
claimed the site a work of art.

Praiseworthy, cried the critics, **priceless**,
and the art scholars concurred;
they lauded the streams steaming out of the pile,
the muck by the drain –
fame came shortly.

Then, aware of her lover's luck,
– the garbage art transcendent –
the telemarketer lost her phone,
promised connections gone in a flash.
Nonetheless, anticipating all, she sings out:
"I've got an artist in my house
I've an artist under my wing."

SILENT DREAMS

I doze in an airport slumber
on a seat not made for sleep;
little dreams or splinters of dreams
visit the dulled chambers of my brain.
An angel nearly strangles
what he sees:

My mother is spanking my bottom
with a brush – letting it fly from an anger
the dream allows.
She cries – I don't,
and the visuals clip off
as the loudspeaker comes on
announcing the flights
and how long before boarding.

I drift back again – there's time –
now it's my wife, my love,
separated by fish and an ocean,
who is being spanked – not with a brush
but by the strong hands of a lover
who aims his right where it knows
what to do, while the left knows as well
but does what it does differently.

These voids between connecting flights
are hours trapped in a crease of time
for the tired traveler;
he longs to be treated as a patient –
kindly, gently, by a tender mother
or mate, and urged back to sanity.

SAYS THE BOY WITH A WART ON HIS NOSE:

The girl around the corner,
has a carbuncle the size of my cheek,
circular, right beneath her left shoulder,
and there is a rumor around town –
Loverlee Massachusetts –
that one day we're bound to wed.

I don't believe it, but Sammy the Mouth,
trustworthy in all ways but math,
tells me it's true - a truth to contemplate.
He points to her fetching ways,
thin ankles, muscular calves,
the sideways smile all of a sudden;
and there's that datebook she keeps.

Lately, no one talks about
her alleged corruption, radiant flesh, her stain;
I see nothing either –
apart from her famous red rise –
and there's no reason to doubt Sammy.

She walked past me the other day
and flashed a look so fast I sat there confused.
Was that out of pity or disdain
for my wart? Or was that a sweet yearning
after my nose and its surrounding self?

I imagine making it into her datebook;
after a date, a touch on the hand, a kiss,
a second date – proper steps toward matrimony –
and then years of settling,
as we sail beyond our blemishes.

SPEAKING OF TANYA

She can cross her legs again
having lost all that weight,
but I'm out of town
and missing nothing I can't afford.
We were friendly years ago
even as she held back on the warmth
that could have swung us along.

I'm back in town now
and Tanya's almost thin,
and her friends say she
could lean in my direction.
What dare I do to renew the alliance?
Call or email, text, or smoke signal?
Would she respond or leave me fretful
and regretful?

Ah, she's seen the puffs
and called my number,
invited me over. I'm dressed
pretty as a school boy rouged up
and ready with a gift to give,
an emblem from a past season
when I went in further than ever
she said back then.

Now she smiles just inches from
my greeting – soon right here now
something's recovered – yes!
All that I thought lost
is so close and open armed.
Is this a mirage, mockery, or miracle?
Chance will tell soon
and time will too.

THE DISPIRITED LOVER

Wondrous it was when love arrived
in late surprise;
its exit trashed the decade's climb

to the crest – where a mossy patch
still grows undisturbed from another season.
Spring water courses downhill

sweetened not by memory
but by what memory denies.
It flows over stones that give nothing

and reminds no one of anything
other than loss and a final touch.
He, despite his internal haze,

still spells the old words
and zips down the line of his fly.
Under the eaves and whipping winds,

the tidy seams of love fray –
"in error" – he cries, wincing.
But woe to him who says

woe is me: there are fatal cases
in earth's infirmary.

HE THINKS OUT LOUD

Remembering those redolent zones
south of the border – the body of a country –
geographically speaking;
it's so humid down there – so many vines
wouldn't dare stay there long
as in a myth or a pornographic lifetime;
but visits, yes – extended occasions
have been salutary – some lasting days.
Much to be, already has been, fathomed,
so I go down there
with no gear to burden the trip,
just my love mood and appetite
scoping out the folds –
"go further south" she whispers.

I will think of her now
not as the one always so humid
she couldn't keep the tops of her socks dry,
nor as the sparrow in heat,
but as the calm wonder with a book - speed-reading
before knocking in a nail,
or cooking up a ragout –
radiant and busy in her sunset rays.

THAT WAS THEN FOREVER

Where am I in your intelligence,
now that you've moved over
and away — living like a banshee,
by the lake with your lovers
both in the pink and you their rose?

For five years our stew simmered.
We talked, basted and added spices;
a taste of all we did
would shame prudence and the devil,
and improve the morals of our tribe.

During our prime of rapt attention,
we pledged "forever" often,
but not thinking of time
our days ran off the clock —
fireflies flown from the jar.

Now, there's little weight left —
near to nothing - lint on a blind man's coat.
We rarely speak — maybe soon never.
However, when I recall that disturbance,
I grieve, grieve and glow — in an instant.

SWIMMING TOWARDS 70

Sally's telling her friend Suzie
about this guy she knows
who months away from 70
finds himself in bed at night
in the semi-dark with a young couple -
the female, not quite 30,
and the he-male a leap year ahead.
They like to play *No Boundary Please,*
he told me that in so many words.

Nearly exhausted, the old guy –
sings aloud while stroking the bed
as if it were a sea,
I'm swimming towards 70,
he said; they laughed a little,
and then turned away
while he kept on swimming.
He's repeated this to me three times already.

Now, two years later
he calls out from another country:
"Sally, I'm swimming towards oblivion –
Where is that famous sight of sand
you spoke of between the sea and safety?"

Suzie, let's pay him a visit
fish him out of the sea
and please him, dry him off
and wrap him in terry cloth.
I'll whisper one comforting thing
and you another – I know
you hardly know him – but it could be sweet:
we'll bring him back.

VANITY

That look on her face:
her head tipped down
so that the eyes peek up
and loiter; eyes like hooks.

Her stare at me
could be a probe into my money
or a considered guess
into my stamina.

In this jazz bar,
single and aghast
that I'm the only one listening,
there's no way not to stare back.

She has an April smile
on this winter's night;
after the piano solo, a shot at heaven,
I start the applause

and don't look around;
when I do, her hands,
previously so still and gathered,
begin to clap and color.

Her face, suddenly brighter
and open to the rhythm,
doesn't look at all uncertain
I'm the one "harmoniously confused"

by her and my lingering vanity.
The piano and drums
set the stage for an impulse of light
that might enter the evening.

DIFFERENT STROKES

He wanted to go out partying
she prefers to stay home with the cat
he wanted to be silly 'till the wee hours
she enjoys home – playing with the cat
he wanted to walk up the hill
she stayed down in the valley
at home with the cat
he wanted to eat out on the dock
she's sickened by the smell of the lake
– prefers home with the cat
he wanted to go fight the Taliban
she despises guns of all kinds,
loves her time at home with cat

then one day his mood shifted
and he gave her a long hard stare –
ran off and joined the fanatics
she remains happy in the company of Mr. Cat.

SALLY TELLS SUZIE ON THEIR WAY

Suzie my dear, stay tight to my side
as we walk, as we go step by step
in a direction you've chosen
passing under an urban arbor,

cruising by the popular locksmith,
the pizza joint, the dirty minded druggist
who already makes us smile; and
we smile again at what we purchase.

Hold my hand in a grip of safety;
we've lots to learn, lots to spend,
time to know each other within the wind,
against the wind, bitter and better.

Last night we hardly knew each other's name,
and it was I who insisted we stay on
after that inconceivable frolic
behind the shrinking twins at the wax museum.

Talk to me as we make our way
the day after a start that had us both finishing,
first you then me – eyes misty.

Lyrics

1. THE DEVIL STRIKES AGAIN

She's got a bright-eyed devil in her pants
she's got a short-assed devil in her pants
feels, she says, like a swarm of ants:
another voice says behave beware
the feelings you have are rich & rare;
he's just a devil, and the devil-may-care.

some time goes by while the music fills

Oh, this joy and uncertainty
her silks a puddle of perplexity
but devil's breath keeps at bay
the sticky freeze,
the chilling breeze,
the bitter bits that make us pray

a little more time goes by

She fingers his velvet horns;
the devil's on her knee telling secrets
this rouster, a bounder, a rooster,
and a boaster too
and then she adds some speed
to her catching fire, her incendiary greed.

2. THE SPLIT AND THE HEALING

You told me I'd be sorry
You told me I'd be grim
swimming beneath your halo
in the land of the Mickey Finn.

You toweled me off,
and led me out –
and spiked my day of leaving;
but the taste on my tongue
was fresh and sweet—
I surely couldn't be leaving,

so I sat awhile, delayed the time
and gained an hour dreaming –
of bulls all froth about to charge
and the boy in the cape side stepping.

You told me I'd be sorry
you told me I'd be blue
living within your favor
in the land of the sometimes true.

Then yards from the door,
minutes from your glow,
beneath the paradise tree,
you broke the spell, the halo's gone
and you've brought us back to us.

A LEAP BEYOND THE TYRANTS

I'm not the devil you imagined
under your sleeve.
One night, despite my sulfurous breath,
you'll invite me in just on the off-chance
that we'll understand all that's malicious
about right-wing terror and defend against it.

We may be enchanted and able to construct
a wall against fire or breakers by the sea
to hold back the bloated tide.
Yes, this love, untested but burgeoning,
will override mere guess-work
and clear the smog belched by the Titans.

They have the cash, the script and the drive,
but our leap beyond stymies their moment,
as we reach for each other
again and again.

Departures

THE CHILD

Old Age: What a silly thing to happen to a little boy.
George Oppen

A child climbs up the old elm,
the ever-living tree,
where snake and tiger
lurk about –
a shield against danger,

limb by limb ascending
into the highest leaves,
where the lawn below resembles desire
to live like the grass – to love long,
to set down seed and die.

TOMORROW

When that lovely word comes true
and the sky bursts to blue,
the shadow that fooled no one lifts,
and we celebrate:
the gold comes teaming –
the morning stretch,
the fresh mouth after the brush
for many – the first coffee or tea.
And then adventure begins
and proves the idea of tomorrow
grander even than luck or love
or holidays with no end of money.

Without tomorrow –as idea or fact:
no hook to hang anything,
no pot to piss in,
no pot no gin,
no kiss from mother, father, wife, or kids,
the old friend who drops by,
the new friend to embrace
and discover her story;
no taste on the tongue
no bitter aftertaste to spit
no failed memory – but to become one.

Banish the thought that blocks the rhythm;
advancing age supports the pretense of wisdom.

EXILE IN OLD AGE

The helicopter lifted off and rose up fast
and then fell and dipped over
and down again and then higher.
I never looked down; I was green
and then white with fear and nausea.

On both sides sat the protectors,
serious and silent.
They set me down on this island
where they promise I'll be
for the rest of my life.

Soon my stomach settled and
my minders cheered up and spoke:
I'm to have food enough and drink
to last my natural lifetime.
Well, I'm old and the planned trip to Kansas

was just a whim, a long shot.
They indicated the storage holds,
the large bins with everything –
but actually – I pointed this out –
 these bins are not so very large.

Then they spoke about madness
and how it thrives in exile.
They suggested the fear –
a subject for a text, they said –
as they lifted up and away.

HIS NOVEMBER

Every inch forward on the going on trail
is one inch closer to the go-no-further –
where the trail is cut off by a ledge.

A crowd of animals – people really –
is pressing close to the edge
where the trail ends and the tale too,
and that's about everything.

IN THE INTERIM

the grief implicit in a grain of sand
is forestalled, not quiet drowned
amidst the voices rising
and then rising higher from the sandbox

small flies settle and rise
off the corpse of a mouse
the greatest action is by the wound
each fly carries its own stigmata

MATURITY

I'll sleep in tomorrow
and as a retired person
with nothing to fill out,
no one to report to,
barely a screw to tighten
or put in a drawer, I'll levitate.

Hours later, I'll come down & nap,
not to prove the license
earned on the high pinnacle of labor,
but because I'm sleepy
& my back feels like a belt
of broken glass.

This doze can come naturally,
but when amplified by chemistry
a millionaire in a hurry
could go broke searching
for this:
a perfect formula.

PRIDEFUL CREATURES

1.
The halo of dust above his eyes
is golden; gold dust at his feet
rises with his step but not too high
to cloud his vision or cause a fall.

Not one insult sullies his calm
or dents the grinning gilded thrall
he's in.

2.
The toad preens on a lily pad;
he basks while the other toads toady;
gold motes speckle the sun.

He imagines yellow a color just for him,
with all the kissing toads about.
And the fish, too, pucker in lust and then love.

The specimen now hops towards the sea;
he owns it all, down to the last ripple.

TAKING NAMES

for Stephen Watson [1954 – 2011]

"There's a Man Going 'Round Taking Names"
African-American spiritual

1.
He makes no money
but His pockets are full.
He sits still with a pal named Patience
taking names;
and then deliberately draws a line.
He runs that line straight through.

Deletions are his thing, we say
a fine thing it is we like to say,
for otherwise the overcrowding,
the countless toes stepped upon,
the misbehavior in the tangled clutches,
the rising stench from every far flung corner
would dull the music and all our preferences:
the taste of salt on tender meat
the taste of wine on the tongue
the sight of a waif, a wave, a wondrous cloud
dropping down the nourishing valley.

2.
But the second part of this bitten cleverness,
this screed on reaping –
the mass swipes or the one by one –
will be brief as time is short:

the mourner bites his nails and his eyes fill
and he cries out loud: "Mister –
who hides in a hood and glides

as if on grease –
this must have been an error
to cross off my handsome friend
in the middle of his everything.
Why this time with that one?"

I plead.

3.
The poet looks around and writes,
as if to a stone,
"God isn't this beautiful:
the fields, the fountains,
the bearded faces and
the smooth dark faces
of the indigenous people,
and the strangers who come to the land
to shoot seed into earth and egg
forever."

The poet, typing up the lush evidence,
disbelieves in this God,
a word with resonance enough,
he pretends, to forestall the name taker
who has no name but God.

MALIGNANT

A spot grows and breeds
and leaves a shadow
inside the lung or the bladder.
From the size of a pea or a dot,
it spirals and takes off like a fickle notion
infiltrating the liver,
the bladder again, and the bowels.

In the heat of a lucky moment
the invaders meet their quotient;
cell-bound they find employment.

Outside the borders,
enemies of the state plot:
at five kilometers and then four,
they toss a rope bridge
to join arms and bodies
with operatives within.
They pray for fire in love with fire.

What to do about the body
invaded by all that activity,
slowed down, bent in captivity?

ELEGY FOR A MAN WHO HADN'T AN EASY GO

for Walter Keller [1937 – 2012]

Walter Keller's in the clink, and it's a long,
longer-than-life sentence – endless.
He did everything plus and nothing at all
to receive such incarceration.

The threads that tie us one to one –
our first breaths to our last –
fray, so sadly,
the ties fray finally.

Walter lies where silence mocks
his previous barking
and all human sound.

SIX SWIPES AT DARKNESS

–the coffee is dead weight in the cup
and with a cold scum afloat

–the hat with its sporty emblem
where is the head to shape the hat?

–the water is low in the cistern
and what's left is wretched

–a small mite on the lower lip
makes a mark and explodes

–someone's son is lost driving at night
met a tree in the dark and sideswiped it

–the train's late; stormy weather on the platform;
standing on the tracks is a windy apparition.

THE SUBJECT

The subject slides under the rug
– not as if swept there –
rather, the subject's ebullient life
drove it in that direction.
It's a bulge now;
press it down repeatedly
and it reappears in a different shape,
a cow or a bull, let's say,
just at the carpet's edge.
Anyone could bend over and gather it up
but not the whole business.
Some bits might cling beneath the rug,
enough for a remark,
enough gas to get to the next pump.

A DANGEROUS DREAM

The darkness lifts,
and I'm awake but not sure;
moth wings whorl under a winter light –
dream-stuff –
their powder drifts like weightless ash –
unknown merit.

A dirty dream came true,
went wrong in the rain,
ran down the gutter and rightly so.

As the season downsized,
the dream-drops froze fast and splintered;
the shards, too small and sharp
to shed light on the dream,
tumbled down the drain.

WRITTEN IN PENCIL

In my pencil is my melody,
sings the sad song drawn to rain.
The drops bead along the window frame
before they fall back into the sea.

Bathers in summertime drive the beach wild
all around the Mediterranean sea,
but a dozen beachcombers,
old in their suits and baggy flesh

are out of it – disallowed from licking salt
off the drying bodies,
so slim but with curves penciled in.
The codgers swim out to the dolphins.

NEVER TO GET THERE

> *That which is in locomotion must arrive at the half-way stage*
> *before it arrives at the goal.*— Aristotle's *Physics*

This is the law of Dichotomy
and – as I perceive – it extends
into all matters physical and political –
splitting halves; a pause at the split.

Arithmetically speaking,
one can never empty the glass
again and again *ad infinitum;*
endless division – as of two minds.

Zeno agrees – Infinite Divisibility:
the distance from the starting mark (S)
to the goal (G) can be divided
into an infinite number of parts.

I muse on halving:
if every move were to hesitate
at the half-way point –
there would be no actual arrival.

Now this snifter was full of fine cognac,
then half and soon down further
to a quarter, a last dram, and then gone.
Gone? Oh, my thirst and the sorry math.

THOUGHTS OF HOME

Home now and clean,
yet cold still and frightened,
the soldier is wrapped
in a blue cotton sheet.
He's been off fighting the enemy
on a military coast.
In this empty room,
neither a warning rings out
nor a reprimand.

             *

Home is where the door unlocks
and the key put aside
and the callused foot bathed
and the heart murmur steadied by a pill;
this is a place in which to lie down
or where, someday,
to place teeth in a glass—
give up moving up
and fanning the sparks.

THE OLD DANCER

He's called the Magic Mover in the theater
and he's billed that way — always.
Photographs show him not yet bent,
but on the way, scratching his pate,
trying to organize a new step
for a new season.

Meanwhile, or in-between shows,
he's busy enough - wall-building, weaving,
corresponding with old lovers,
whose flames burned and melted
beside his quickstep,
his graceful inside turn.

He can still sail in the music,
ebullient, light of tread and/or sharp of accent
and nail the moment;
but there have been rumors enough
to blemish his name —
had the news caught on.

Nowadays and nights, in this last lingering while,
he's a five minute dancer at the Cool Spot café.
Whatever the audience, he's on nightly
right in step, twisting with the swirling skirts,
almost equal to every measure,
adequate to nearly every swirl.

Lyrics

I. FOR JOHN HICKS 1942-2006

John's gone
but here comes John
take me with the 12 beats
take me with the 5
take me with the 12 beats
take me with the 5
bring him back to live.

John ...
hear his full-bodied laughter ...
no, I can't hear it well enough
to bring him back.

"Rum & coke and spice of lime
is all I'm taking in" –
a lyric John could have sung
had he lied.

"I've been cleansed since;
the doctors of science
some with love in their pockets too
have been at my side and closer too,

but all those years of taking in
have now put me out.
It's too late to retrace a step
take back a sip

or fix myself differently
how could I,
how could you
so distant from where I am?"

2. THE FAREWELL TRIO ON TUESDAYS

The gate was slim,
but for one devoté – also slim –
sitting up front and still,
while the staff – short-handed this night –
shifted about – adjusting the lights and sound.

Farewell – a fare-thee-well to see through.
The come-on was a ploy from the start,
a practiced kiss goodbye,
never to be tossed – the trio says –
as they mount the bandstand.

John adjusts his seat, focuses and hits a G 7;
Wilber's bass is up-right, while Billy
brushes the drums maybe twice –
and John's right hand introduces,
"Detour Ahead" in C minor.

If this music – earth born and heaven sent –
should ever be a final performance,
make the minutes so fractioned
that they swell with silver and fill with gold
into channels of forever.

PLEASE, LISTEN TO THE MUSIC

When you come to my door
with that original smile,
wielding a bat with a smasharoo,
please do your damage
between noon and twilight,
time enough to change the day,
improve the outlook – for us both.

Please, at the end of my story –
a lament over slaughter,
explosions, slips of order,
background music to all past wars –
don't say, "small potatoes,"
and if you must mutter warnings,
let them come true but slowly.

Please be quiet down at the bar
with the music only measures away.
Piano, bass, drum and horn all hold
the echoes and the portents;
"The horror, the horror" – a drunk stutters –
and the jazzman says,
"compared to what?"

THE FINALE

It's not over 'till it's over
thinks the pitcher about to pitch
in the 11th inning –
the fat lady's not even in the house
and there's a chance;
but
says the trumpet
in the middle of the cadenza –
"sometimes it's over even before it's over,"
and the band plays on
and the ballgame bounces along
as if time itself could erase the finale
which had already fallen on both.

Sometimes it's long past bedtime
before the child closes her eyes.

TONY'S GHOSTS

Tony's lost a friend again,
thus the hole in his halo,
the plugs in his heart that fail
to allow the new loss in.
He cannot even spell the ghost's name.
Other holes, less visible but there,
polka-dot 'round his head.

The news of this latest ghost
to play on the field
came from dispirited souls
who lived on the other side
of some mild issue.
Minimalist Tony has stayed away.
At his best, he catches shadows
crossing the street
even on days without sunlight.

TONY'S RETURN

Scuffling slantwise on a climb up the stairwell,
stories of his eldership
clock his breathing.
He's making more mistakes than before,
sometimes on purpose, to provide his mark
a reason to remember
a long-ago slip,
one that made him move faster that night.

Fix the logic, he says in his mind,
but his brain, always ruled by his groin,
is swollen with all those slip-ups
on the way upstairs.
Stricken by years, he babbles,
as a tear falls on his sleeve.
When I'm gone – he says –
there'll be one less shadow on the pavement.

WHAT WAS, WAS

My father, no longer cold in his coffin
but returning to dust,
as the coffin too will do in time,
liked to say in old age
with a thinned-out smile
"what was, was"
and it had a sweet ring
when applied to a thing –
the dishwasher done-in finally
and a replacement on its way,
an LP recording now on CD,
an auto gone to rust and
money down on a shiny one;
a nasty remark finally forgotten.

What was, was:
an old bird fallen off its wing
leaves of autumn
a tear that's dried
a full head of hair
now thinned to a shine
the body's waste –
flushed away as this music fades:
a practice for the end
that does not does not come;
the music does not stop.

For every *was* in time's fast memory,
an *is* trumps the was every time.

ABOUT THE AUTHOR

Barry Wallenstein is a former professor of literature and writing at the City University of New York and an editor of the journal, *American Book Review*. During his tenure at City College, he founded and directed the Poetry Outreach Center and edited the journal *Poetry in Performance*. His earliest poems appeared in 1964 and since then he has published eight collections. Most recent is an English/French bilingual edition entitled *Tony's Blues*. In the early 1970's he began performing and recording with jazz artists, establishing long term relationships with renowned musicians, including saxophonist, Charles Tyler, bassists Massimo Cavalli and Ken Filiano, pianists John Hicks and Adam Birnbaum, and French horn player, Vincent Chancey. He continues to perform with musicians internationally. He lives in New York City.

[Website: www.barrywallenstein.com]